No Longer Fading

No Longer Fading

Cover design by Eric St. Clair

Front artwork by Steph Newell

No Longer Fading

by

Eric St. Clair

Artwork by

Steph Newell

No Longer Fading

© 2010 by Eric St. Clair

St. Clair Publications

All rights reserved. No part of this publication may be reproduced or transmitted in any form by any means electronic or mechanical, including telecopy, recording, or any information storage and retrieval system now known or invented, without permission in writing from the publisher, except by a reviewer who wishes to quote brief passages in connection with a review written for inclusion in a magazine, newspaper or broadcast.

ISBN 978-0-9826302-7-3

Printed in the United States of America by

St. Clair Publications

P. O. Box 726

Mc Minnville, TN 37111-0726

http://stan.stclair.net

TABLE OF CONTENTS

Under Your Gaze	9
Overcome Once Again	11
My Love	13
Killing the Liar	15
Redemption	17
No Longer Fading	19
Words and Names	21
Secret Knowledge of Creation	23
Rage	25
Light Fades	27
Lost Things	29
Parade	31
Beautiful One	33
Wasteland	35
Pieces	37
Monk	39
EL	41
Pabbi	43

Flows from the Heart	**45**
About the Author	**46**

No Longer Fading

No Longer Fading

Under Your Gaze

Your gaze upon me shines like rays of sun bending around the bare branches of a mighty oak on a dying winter day.

It comes with the gentle warmth that the winter sun inevitably brings. My leafless limbs tingle at the life your gaze brings.

I feel you have so much more you want to give. Much more than this gentle warmth affords.

I begin to realize that in my bare and leafless state I could never endure the fullness of your gaze. So you patiently wait for me day after day.

I can feel your growing warmth resting on my frame. I drink from the life your showers bring, my roots grow deep.

Your gaze is always there. It is a comfort to budding fruit hanging so gently from these oaken limbs.

Under your gaze my branches hang with the sweet fruit of your love.

Under your gaze I will continue to die and grow… to die and grow….

Reykjavik, Iceland

16 June 2009

No Longer Fading

No Longer Fading

Overcome Once Again.

Head thrown back. My arms outreached. I am so lost in you! My skin is tingling, my body jerking. The way you fill me is so intense. You leave me feeling like my skin has been turned inside out. My heart beats so freely for all to see. In this moment you are all I need. You´ve left me spent, but strangely refreshed and revived. I have been drained of all but you. So I stumble out into the night, numb to all but this feeling. Overcome once again by you…

Reykjavík, Iceland

18 June 2009

No Longer Fading

No Longer Fading

My Love

You are creation. Brilliant and gleaming. Your heart too big for one human to hold. It bursts at every seam. Your thoughts are grand, deep and dark. The eyes to your soul are covered with broken and dirty lenses. Your soul is too big for one human to carry. Why can´t you see, oh creation, that you are brilliant and gleaming, shining with the beauty of Zion? Why don´t you see the healing that comes from the touch of your hand? Oh brilliant and gleaming creation, I stand here beside you. Waiting and watching. Holding my breath to see where your freedom takes you….

Reykjavík, Iceland

21 June 2009

No Longer Fading

No Longer Fading

Killing the Liar

I must kill this liar that rests within. Today I take an axe and I begin to chop. With each blow I tear down strongholds. Cutting out this poison will be the only way I can live. For so long I looked to the liar for identity and protection. Liar, you left me an empty, deflated shell of the man I am meant to be. So today I stand with axe in hand. Here I am world, one man broken and weak. And I am OK with that!

Reykjavík, Iceland

22 June 2009

No Longer Fading

Redemption

Redemption takes time. It must be walked out step by step by painful, glorious step. I cannot be sure when my redemption occurred. But oh do I know when it began. It started with me standing before the Creator. Stripped bare to the nakedness of my soul. This nakedness was not to shame me. But for redemption, I had to leave all behind. Stripped of all the hiding places that kept me bound to a prison of self hate and deprecation. Somewhere on this path to redemption I passed myself in the night. A shadowy figure hunched over from the weight of this world. I tried to slide by without being noticed. But as I passed he caught my eye. The pain in his eyes and the hurt in his soul screamed to me without saying a word. Keep going! Keep walking! Don´t stop! This walk of redemption will save us. So I walk. Step by step by painful, glorious step.

Reykjavík, Iceland

22 June 2009

No Longer Fading

No Longer Fading

I´ve been untwisted. I´m no longer fading.

You´ve grabbed the tattered string and unraveled me from deep within.

Taken to depths that my heart cannot believe.

Inhaling air that almost burns to breath.

I stand before you, no longer fading.

I´m untwisted and unraveled.

Wrapped in your depth, so alive and finally breathing.

Reykjavík, Iceland

29 June 2009

No Longer Fading

No Longer Fading

Words and Names

Words and names are alive and breathing.

We take them on and give them life.

Sticks and stones? Yea, they broke my bones.

But oh how the words and names piled up and eventually crushed me.

Then you came along.

You picked these words and names off one by one.

You helped me up and dusted me off.

You gave me a new name, and filled my heart with beautiful words of life.

Reykjavík, Iceland

29 June 2009

No Longer Fading

Secret Knowledge of Creation

Your eyes, oh how they gleamed, I loved the way they twinkled.

I will never forget the way you would stop to smell flowers.

You inhaled them just so. Like you had a secret knowledge of their role in creation.

You were my friend and you loved me so freely.

I cried last night when they told me you died.

So, today as I walked and thought of you, I knelt in the grass and I smelled a flower.

Hoping to find the secret knowledge of its role in creation.

Kneeling there, all I found were tears!

I will miss you my friend!

Reykjavík Iceland

29 June 2009

No Longer Fading

Rage

Rage is a complicated thing to comprehend when you're 9 years of age. So it gets pushed down and pushed down and numbed down to hate. After many years the hate turns to anger and then somewhere along the way just becomes numbness. Many years later when it seems safe, the lid is slowly pulled back. The memories are flooded with oxygen and light. The rage returns and turns to anger and subsides in sadness and tears. Then I notice the 9-year-old, too young to have been left to be ravaged and broken. I see him tilt his face to the light and he takes a deep breath and smiles. He has finally been freed. I am no longer angry. I am no longer filled with rage. I tilt my face to the light and I begin to breathe. I smile at my own new-found freedom.

Reykjavik, Iceland

20 July 2009

No Longer Fading

No Longer Fading

Light Fades

Standing here in the harbor and the wind hits my face. It´s not a very cold wind, but cold enough to remind me of much colder days. The endless light is fading as the days once again begin to share with the night. I am trying hard to fight the sadness that is trying so hard to settle in. One should not think about the death of a season when it is still so full of life, but when this eternal light fades there is just so much night.

Reykjavik, Iceland

23 July 2009

No Longer Fading

No Longer Fading

Lost Things

Sitting here thinking. Thinking of things I have lost. Some things were taken. Some were given away and others just plain gone. Some of these I held too close, and for my own freedom had to let them go. Some were taken by force, ripped from my tight-clinched fingers. Taken through pain, suffering and bleeding. But not you! You were the easiest thing I ever let go! Strange to see now what it would have cost me to keep you. I am glad I lost you and I am so overwhelmed by the love I have found.

Reykjavik, Iceland

4 August 2009

No Longer Fading

No Longer Fading

Parade

    The rain has come and the streets are sticky with the remains of streamers and confetti. The parade is over and the people are leaving. I have marched down your streets. I have danced and I have sung. I have played every part that I could imagine to play. The parade is over and the people are leaving. My legs too tired to dance and my voice too sore for singing. They all hurry on to catch the next fools' parade. Now I walk down your streets; there is a slight limp to my step. I am fine with it, though. It reminds me of the parade and all of the people. I am alive now and I have just started dreaming.

    Reykjavik Iceland

    6 August 2009

No Longer Fading

Beautiful One

    Oh, beautiful one. I wish I could have been there when you were born. To see you before you were battered, torn, pushed away and labeled as broken. Yes, pure friend, I wish we could have spoken before all the baggage. To see your light shine from an unaltered package. You were pushed down, held down, and force-fed false notions. You were left to float along on other men's oceans. These notions you've been fed, and this identity that you've been carrying, are too heavy to hold and they have become a cold prison. Identity is just perception of who we've become, but, my love, don't ever confuse that with who you are. Your name is pure, friend, and your heart shines with the brilliance of the Sun. Let go of identity and break free from the prison! Arise from the ashes! Fight! Fight! Fight! Until you have fully risen!

    Reykjavik, Iceland

    28 August 2009

No Longer Fading

No Longer Fading

Wasteland

    I stand in this vast wasteland. A land strewn with the remains of great warriors who have passed this way before me. Warriors who died striving for greatness. Seeking to take this land as a testament to their glory and power. The warriors were crushed and broken. Their blood flowing in the cracks of this scorched desert land. So here I stand in this vast wasteland, with a thousand warrior-angels at my guard. My steps are sure. My eyes are continuously straining on the horizon. Looking towards the King. Inching across this wasteland, straight into the arms of my glorious King.

    Reykjavik, Iceland

    31 August 2009

No Longer Fading

No Longer Fading

Pieces

I love to watch you move. The way you slide through a room awakens such incredible emotions deep within. You view the world with an innocence that comes from some hidden place that has escaped the brokenness of our daily lives. You see the world through a beautiful fractured prism of light. You see life bathed in colors that are brilliant and gleaming. You see me in ways that I could never see myself. You don´t always see the puzzle but you painstakingly care for each of the pieces. Carrying them bundled over your shoulder. Eagerly and gracefully moving ahead with a resolute resignation that it is your burden to carry. I watch you slide through the room and I am left dreaming of seeing the brilliant colors of these beautiful and painstakingly-bundled up pieces.

Reykjavík, Iceland

21 September 2009

No Longer Fading

Monk

When I was a kid you seemed to tower above all of life. You were a bear of a man. Arms and hands strong from a lifetime of labor. Skin stained from years of toiling under the sun. As I grew older I saw you through the eyes of others. Friend, husband, father, and brother. As a friend you were the most loyal of loyal. As a husband you took such gentle care of your dying wife and spoke to her with such incredible respect. As a father you loved all your children just the way they needed. You were hard but fair, and always forgiving. As a brother I saw you care for each of your siblings with such love, as they each slowly passed. I knew you as many things. Friend, sage, confidant, and nurturer. You took time to answer all of my ridiculously unending questions. We went on long walks and you would share with me the wisdom you gleaned from almost a century of living. You shared with me things that were deep in your heart and always listened so intently when I bared to you my soul. You encouraged me and always believed in me even when I did not believe in myself. You were a good man and my grandfather. I still miss you every day.

Reykjavík, Iceland

21 September 2009

No Longer Fading

No Longer Fading

EL

I am so weak! I have convinced myself of your elusiveness. That this distance between us is who you are. The truth though is dark and insidious. The truth is that I am selfish. It is said that you wrap yourself in light. I wrap myself in layer upon layer of self gratification. An endless ravel of constant diversion. This distance between us is immeasurable and crushing. Why can't I choose you? Why can't I break these chains that bind me? How long must this distance stand between us? I need to feel you now, safely clinched in your embrace. Remove this darkness from my heart. Fill me with your beautiful healing light.

Reykjavík Iceland

22 September 2009

No Longer Fading

Pabbi

It is 1978 and I am six years of age. As I walk through the yard I see him building. Stacking stone upon stone. He seemed so indestructible, with hands as strong as steel. He was like a superhero in this six-year-old's eyes, minus the tights and the cape, of course. I loved the weekends because he was always home. During the week I would wait for him to pull into the drive. My hero was home, and everything would be fine. I am not sure what happened over the years to come. I began to see the man for who he was. Or at least my perception of who I thought he was. I began to see the cracks in the armor. I saw hands not much stronger than mine. I saw a man--- just a man. I resented him for not being the superhero that I had created. Now the years have moved on and I am two decades older than the man I saw stacking stones in the yard. Somewhere along the way I lost my superhero, but I gained a friend. I now see a man who strains to lift stones. Far too often left breathless and weak. I see hands that are not that strong anymore. But I am moved by a man who is still becoming. Never stopping his search of becoming the man he was meant to be. It has been a pleasure to see him rise. He is an amazing father, an incredible friend and a super man.

Reykjavik, Iceland

21 October 2009

No Longer Fading

Flows from the Heart

They say poetry flows from the heart.

It is a relief to know my hands and my mouth have not failed me.

Oh, but my heart is betraying me!

Shutting down.

The words no longer flow.

They come drip… drip…. Dripping… trickling in one by one.

Twisted and out of order.

I need you!

I need you to come and kick start my heart.

I need the words to flow again.

Reykjavík, Iceland

10 December 2009

About the Author

Eric St. Clair was born in Blacksburg, Virginia, and reared in Charlotte, North Carolina. He and his wife of fifteen years, Katie, have lived in Reykjavik, Iceland for the past two and a half years. Eric owns his own music business, is a theologian, and is part of the group *24/7 Prayer*.

www.ingramcontent.com/pod-product-compliance
Lightning Source LLC
Chambersburg PA
CBHW041526090426

42736CB00035B/31